ANN MORRIS

WORK

LOTHROP, LEE & SHEPARD BOOKS • MORROW

NEW YORK

The author wishes to thank Woodfin Camp & Associates and the following photographers who have contributed photographs to this book: Nubar Aexanian, p. 7; Marc and Evelyne Bernheim, pp. 8 (right), 10 (top); Bernard Boutrit, p. 16; Robert Frerck, pp. 19 (top), 23; Michael Heron, p. 11 (top); Ken Heyman, pp. 5, 6, 8 (left), 10 (bottom), 12, 26, 27; Yva Momatiuk and John Eastcott, pp. 2, 13 (left), 18, 19 (bottom), 25/front jacket; Kal Muller, pp. 1, 9, 15; Betty Press, pp. 13 (right), 14, 22, 28, 29; L. Schirmer, pp. 20, 21; Mike Yamashita, p. 17. The photograph on the bottom of page 11 is by Ann Morris.

Published by Lothrop, Lee & Shepard Books
an imprint of Morrow Junior Books
a division of William Morrow and Company, Inc.
1350 Avenue of the Americas, New York, NY 10019
http://www.williammorrow.com

Printed in Hong Kong by South China Printing Company (1988) Ltd.

1 2 3 4 5 6 7 8 9 10

Library of Congress Cataloging-in-Publication Data
Morris, Ann.
Work/Ann Morris.
p. cm.
Summary: Photographs and brief text show people all over the world at work.
ISBN 0-688-14866-2 (trade)—ISBN 0-688-14867-0 (library)
1. Work—Juvenile literature. [1. Work.] II. Title.
HD4902.5.M59 1998 306.3'6—dc21 97-21607 CIP AC

WORK

All over the world,

people work . . .

mommies work

daddies work

and children work, too.

13

16   and together,

at home

and away from home.

They use their muscles

and their minds.

People work hard
to get the job done right.

Work can make you tired,

but work can make you
feel good, too!

INDEX

14 TOGO: A seamstress makes sure the dress she has sewn is the right size by fitting it on a wooden dressmaker's dummy.

15 MYANMAR: This young Buddhist monk likes going to the well to draw fresh water for his monastery. Who wouldn't want to run an errand outdoors on a sunny day?

16 FRANCE: Customers line up to buy the delicious cheeses and other good things for sale at this food stall in the covered market in Royan.

17 UNITED KINGDOM: These field-workers are harvesting narcissus on a farm in Lincolnshire.

18 CANADA: Every member of the Lien family pitches in to take care of their farm animals and pets.

19 NEW ZEALAND: Many people enjoy working in their gardens. This mother and daughter are weeding the flower beds outside their Queenstown home.

19 CHINA: The members of this farm family in Yunnan Province are husking corn to be ground into food for their pigs.

20 GERMANY: It takes many people working together to fly a commercial airplane. This pilot and his crew are preparing to take off from Schönefeld Airport in Berlin.

22 TOGO: This young man is learning to become a carpenter. He is using a tool called a plane to make the surface of a board smooth and even.

23 MEXICO: The reading, writing, and math skills this executive worked hard to master in school now help her run a company.

25 CHINA: This young monk studies hard so that someday he will have the knowledge necessary to read and interpret the sutras—a collection of sacred Buddhist writings.

26 PANAMA: In many warm countries, people stop working and take a siesta during the hottest part of the day.

27 PORTUGAL: After a long day at market, this young boy counts the vegetables to see how many he has sold.

28 KENYA: These members of the Mathare Youth Sports Association have volunteered to help clean up their neighborhood, one of the poorest sections of the capital city of Nairobi.

Where in the world were these photographs taken?

Canada

NORTH
AMERICA

United States

PACIFIC
OCEAN

Mexico

CENTRAL AMERICA

Panama

SOUTH
AMERICA

ATLANTIC
OCEAN

Germany

England
(United Kingdom)

France

Portugal

EUROPE

ASIA

AFRICA

Israel

Egypt

Ivory
Coast

Togo

Kenya

China

India

Myanmar

INDIAN
OCEAN

PACIFIC
OCEAN

AUSTRALIA

New Zealand